BE HAPPY

ANANDO BRAHMA.

VENKATA CHALAM RALLAPALLI

Made with ♥ on the Notion Press Platform
www.notionpress.com

Contents

CHAPTER ONE

Where is happiness?

If you observe any child ... the child is always cheerful and full of vibrant zeal and enthusiasm.

A child is inquisitive and lives in the present and enjoys every moment of life irrespective of any other materialistic possessions, notwithstanding any fame or wealth, etc.

Though the grown-up individual is much stronger, intelligent, and resourceful... he is always generally not as cheerful as a child. Why? Why can't an adult be as cheerful as a child, if not more?

Is the weight of more knowledge, awareness, and power results in more burden and ultimate unhappiness?

What prevents human beings from enjoying the present and living happily to its full extent?

Why the present generation is living in perpetual stress, strain, mental agony, and unhappiness, without ever realizing true happiness, which is the basic and innate nature of human beings?

Why we are not able to laugh or be cheerful, which is a unique privilege given to human beings, unlike animals or plants?

These are the general doubts, every person will get, in the mundane journey of life.

Our ancestors and learned monks have experienced this dilemma, and they have shown us the path of happiness and eternal peace, to enjoy this gift called human life. Only thing is, we have forgotten our culture and ignored the Vedic knowledge as rubbish and adopted modern concepts, and living in eternal crisis, in the pursuit of real happiness.

After experiencing the same situation in middle age and other trials and tribulations, I have started exploring the solution for this problem, and the result is this small book, which explains the process.

The genesis of the problem:

Why a person is always seem to be unhappy despite his wealth, fame, or riches?

Why human beings are always craving money and material wealth and running after earthy possessions

paying a heavy price in the bargain?

Are we exchanging our age-old blissful way of slow life, ethos, culture, and customs for the western lifestyle, which is more materialistic and full of the pursuit of happiness and whether we can get the desired results or not?

Why do the ancestors of our bullock cart age and without any modern gadgets and comforts, seem to be happier and healthy than us, despite having more money, comforts, and gadgets now?

These are some of the questions that have been haunting me since my college days. I have been persistently seeking answers to the above-cited questions from learned professors, teachers, self-styled babas, and all the books I could be able to read and refer to.

Only after going through" the BHAGAVAD GITA" and after reading and listening to many scholarly interpretations of the book only, I could get more convincing and realistic answers to the above questions.

I realized, rather late, that The Geeta is not a religious book, but it is a book that teaches us how to conduct our lives and what is our inner personality.

My own life lessons and more turbulent events in my private and public life have taught me various lessons, and I continue to be an ardent student forever in this real-life university.

I would like to share my insights and my perspective on the world, which may throw some light on many people, who are also having the same unanswered question about how to be cheerful and happy.

CHAPTER TWO

Genesis of happiness

As many learned people state, HAPPINESS IS A STATE OF MIND.

Happiness is always created within you and may be reflected outside.

If you don't have inner happiness, you can not afford it in the outside world, however rich you may be.

What is the genesis of happiness? WE. YES ... WE. ...

Our thoughts, our outlook, our belief system, our way of looking at things, our way of mental conditioning, and our inner personality.

We link pain or pleasure to any thought or action and thereby we are the genesis and cause of either happiness or unhappiness, whatsoever may be the outward reasons or labels we use.

There is a clear connection between the happy-inducing nerve centres and the brain impulses that will be transformed into happiness. As it is possible to link happiness or unhappiness to anything, our thoughts or actions will be the source and responsible for our happiness and bliss.

IF YOU UNDERSTAND THIS,

WE START REFRAMING OUR THOUGHTS BY LIKING **WHAT WE DO, INSTEAD OF ETERNALLY WAITING FOR DOING WHAT WE LIKE.**

If we start liking our daily activities, then there is no stress either in the job or professional activity or in the day-to-day routine chores, which we are bound to do, to meet both ends meet.

Similarly, many of the keys that open the world of happiness are very simple and basic.

But, it is very difficult to change our beliefs, convictions, perceptions, and social and mental conditioning, preventing us from enjoying eternal and abundant happiness.

What are the various tools, techniques, and routines, we have to follow or religiously adhere to overcome the above hurdles and show the path to a stress-free life and eternal bliss, which will be discussed in the following chapters?

CHAPTER THREE

HAPPINESS IS A CHOICE

If at all, if there is anybody in the world who can make you happy and give the promise to bestow you with eternal happiness, that is possible with only one person... **that is YOU only.**

You alone can bring about the necessary changes in your inner personality and resolve yourself that

whatever may be the situation, happiness is my choice.

Nobody can make you unhappy, without your consent.

It is your belief system, not ordinary belief ... but a burning desire to change your life, that is going to make a difference in the world.

It is not fate or your birth star or Vaastu or destiny that is going to decide your happiness. It is your thinking and belief system.

This is precisely what we have to focus on...

To focus on the sources of happiness or unhappiness. What is the cause, and what is our reaction?

What makes you happy, or what is that preventing you from happiness? It is the daily analysis, observation and if possible, maintaining a written note... that will create a better understanding of our inner feelings, our emotional state and our thought process.

It creates a real measurement of our state of mind. What is our thought process? What is triggering the unhappiness or sources of dissatisfaction or frustration?

It is understanding of your mind, analysis of your emotions and trigger points of unhappiness that will give you a clue of what action is to be taken to control the source of dissatisfaction or unhappiness.

Mere knowledge without any action is useless. At the same token, any action or reaction without any requisite knowledge is also an empty exercise.

It is a real paradigm shift and epoch-making day when you decide to change yourself to enjoy every moment of life.

You have to decide and take a firm resolution that " I AM NOT GOING TO BE INFLUENCED BY EXTERNAL INFLUENCES OR CONDITIONS, TO MAKE ME HAPPY. "

Remember that you have to take a stand that nobody is responsible or accountable for your state of happiness. You will not give any chance to external people or situations, to rob your peace of mind or harmony.

Note that You can tune your brain either to be happy or unhappy.

Furthermore, you can give auto suggestions to your subconscious mind by repeating the positive affirmations of happiness state until it becomes second nature. You can choose to be happy and be positive, even in the worst challenging situations and in the company of negative people also.

This is the magic mantra or rigorous principle, which may be mastered by anybody, by constant practice and persisting with the " control of the mind" throughout your life.

CHAPTER FOUR

DIAGNOSIS OR INVESTIGATION OF SOURCE OF UNHAPPINESS

For finding a solution or to give a prescription for any disease, we have to find out the root cause or investigate the reasons and find out the various negative factors contributing or source of unhappiness.

Once the correct diagnosis is done, half of the battle is won.

We may say that unhappiness or our troubles are due to the following general factors.

1. GENERIC IN NATURE, LIKE COMPARISON, FEELING, PERCEPTION ETC.

2.MIND RELATED

3. PHYSICAL BODY RELATED

4.OTHERS.. WHICH CAN NOT BE PIN POINTED like mixed reasons

We are not much focussed on unhappiness related to the physical body related troubles as some may have some congenial defects, or may be suffering from vocational hazards, or nutrition deficiency related or lifestyle related problems. It has a other medical related dimension and treatment by the doctors and medical fraternity.

We are only concerned and focussed on the people who are otherwise physically fit, leading an absolutely normal life, and they are leading their normally. But, still they are unhappy because of their mental attitude, belief system, mental makeup and brought up etc.

In other words, we are also bothered about the people who are blessed with all the good things in life, still they always show the sign of frustration, defeat, low self honor etc. and they live in a state of confusion and perpetual fear of some unknown fear or future.

These type of people always live in the past or future and never live in the present. They have unknown fears, always live in perpetual tension about future, blame others for their present state.

These people are the right people, who can be transformed into peaceful, cheerful persons, by changing their thinking and their daily rituals and actions.

They can be mentored or by practice, they can be more stable emotionally and make them understand that the trouble is with your attitude and way of thinking.

CHAPTER FIVE

HABITS AND SUB-CONSCIOUS

Habit is an act which we will do repeatedly and routinely without much effort and unconsciously also at times. IT is formed by repeating an act several times until we can do it without our presence of mind. Over a period, say 3 weeks or maximum 2 to 3 months, any action or routine will become a habit and unconsciously, we can do it, or we are forced to do it, without much pain or resistance.

Hence, we have to cultivate the daily routine or program our brain in realizing the acts which trigger happiness, and we have the ability to associate the pleasure or happiness to this routine action, however difficult it is, while doing so.

To give an example, a morning walk in the early morning may be difficult initially.

If we persist for 21 days, without any break, we may change our initial resistance or unhappiness state of mind into either non-resistance and after some more period, we may realize the benefits of walking and start enjoying it.

What transformed it.? The perseverance or persistence with good habits, which may be difficult initially but very beneficial and good after continuous practice.

Hence, the happiness or unhappiness exists in our thinking, or attitude but not in the actual act or thing per se. Same thing or action may be a cause of happiness for one person, whereas it may be an unhappy thing for another, basing on how you look at it or how you are perceiving it.

Have you ever prepared a list of acts or things which will instantly brings you happiness or at least change your mood?

Have ever tried to change your mood by changing your pattern of behavior or thought process? If you continue to do the same thing or following the same pattern of action, the result will be the same. You can not expect an apple by sowing a mango seed.

Similarly, if you sow an unhappy seed and expecting a bliss and happy result, you are asking for disappointment.

Unfortunately, many people expect miracles or live in an eternal mirage that something will change suddenly or by magic, and somebody will come and wipe out their entire suffering.

Nothing will ever change, unless you would make it. No destiny or no star would change your bad situation into the best situation, by its own. There is no magic wand. **No "Mantra" will make you rich or happy, all of a sudden.**

So what we have to do? We have to look internally or within ourselves to find the path of happiness.

Your inward journey or changing your mind, behavior, habits etc. will make a difference.

Whenever we are experiencing any gloominess or being depressed, we have to make conscious effort to change the situation or do something necessary to make amends. No other person, will do it for you.

We may have to make an honest effort, which may take some time to get the desired result, consistently until, we start realizing the rewards of our efforts, in changing the bad to good or unpleasant to at least neutral situation.

For some people, it may be a small change in their daily activity, like going for a walk, listening to the music, or chatting over phone or mobile... Which may instantly bring change in their mental frame, and whatever seemed to be gloomy or depressing will turn out to be rosy and cheerful.

When your mind is capable of linking happiness or unhappiness to any action or incident, why not we try to change it for better and for our perpetual good mood.

The aroma of cooked mutton may be quite enticing and alluring for a Non-vegetarian person, whereas the same food may be allergic or source of vomiting for a vegetarian, who can not even tolerate the thought of presence of small piece of mutton, in his food.

Where is the trick. ? your thinking your belief system... your subconscious mind links or triggers some reaction as either good or bad, basing on its memory or track record or history.

So, the learning point is, with conscious effort and sincere approach, we can make any event or incident as enjoyable or pleasant. It requires some practice, some belief, some sort of persistence, before we get the real fruits of your actions or efforts.

Do it, and repeat it , until you change your mind set.

CHAPTER SIX

Broad Types of People as per nature

As per the teachings of the Bhagavad geeta, people can be broadly divided into three broad categories as per their innate nature or " GUNAs"

1. SATVIK 2 RAJASIK 3 TAMASIK

TAMASIK:

The people falling under this category are considered to be the lowest category, where there is no action or response for any situation.

Total inertia or total ignorance or total indifference to the ground realities of life, and they have no intention of taking any action.

They are lazy, indifferent, and inactive people. They enjoy laziness, they enjoy total indifferent attitude and not bothered about anything.

RAJASIK:

These people are always seems to be in action, and they always agitated.

They are either busy in some worldly acquisitions or running after money, power and other materialistic pursuits. They are constantly in action and never find a moment of peace and solitude. They will not satisfy with the present state of their living and always in a hurry or busy to acquire more and more of every thing, which may land them ultimately in constant stress and confusion.

SAATVIK:

The people, who are to be categorized as " Swastikas" are few in the world, and they seem to be in control of every thing, in all situations. They enjoy balance of life, and they are not in a blind race for power or fame.

These people are peace loving and by nature they are calm and able to control their emotions. They eat saatvik food, and they talk in pleasant manner and their actions are always resulting in peace and harmony.

It is difficult to classify all the people exactly in the different compartments basing on their nature. There may be people with a fair mix of two or three gunas. People may be borne with Rajasik character, but they may transform themselves to be Satvik, after passing of time and age.

Hence, there will be a mix of three gunas also in one person, but in order to classify a person as a Tamas or Rajasik, or Saatvik.. We have to test his dominant character and guna, which dominates or dictates his majority of his life. How, he reacts in a difficult situation. How he acts and talks, when faced with adverse circumstances. That is an acid test, to differentiate the Gunas.

Why this " 3 gunas" reference here?

The innate nature or basic character of a person decides your level of agitation or stress. Your state of well-being internally.

As long as you are pursuing the path of Rajasa, or path of acquisition and enjoyment of wealth, fame or name, you are bound to be in agitated condition and which may result in stress, if it is beyond control.

You can not get total happiness and enjoy the total success in the materialistic world at the same time. You can ride on two horses at a time. You have to sacrifice something for the sake of the other.

AS long as you are linking happiness with something which is going to be acquired in the future, you are bound to be in anxiety and stress. You are more worried about the end result, and you are not able to focus on the present state. Then, it is bound to

result in loss of peace and anxiety.

The Rajasik type people are bound to experience this state of anxiety and stress, because by nature they are very ambitious, interested to acquire more and more money and fame, more action oriented and constantly in a race for more and more power, status, name and fame in the society. They are ever ready to trade their comfort and peace of mind, for the sake of few more luxuries and good things of life.

The sad part of their story is they are not aware of this fact, until it is too late. They never find time to go the self introspection to find out what is the root cause of their continuous stress and anxiety.

These Rajasik people love to be in the state of busy or action, no matter, how much price they pay for it.

They are not aware of their emotions or inner strengths or weaknesses. The best part is, they are not at all bothered to learn.

It mostly resembles the western culture, where money and power is the ultimate objective of the life.

The Thamasik :

Here are people, who are totally opposite to the nature of " Rajasiks". These people are lazy, take things very easy, laid-back, inactive and never interested in any kind of hectic active. They are very sluggish in nature and enjoys long weekends and take their own time to react.

Their food habits are also resonates with their nature. They love eating too much of non-organic or processed food and generally prefers to consume frozen or packed food, to save the trouble of cooking or prepare fresh food.

The stale food, the inactive and their passive nature results in total mess and unorganised life style. Due to their laid back nature and indifferent mental attitude, they lose the opportunities and suffer. They are too lazy to take any positive action to come out of the troubles or change their mindset. They are often obese and blame the society for their misery and failures. They never take any responsibility for their own

mistakes or laziness.

These people, even though, life has given many warnings and chances to mend their ways, enjoy the same lazy routine and ultimately, their inaction and indifferent attitude will result in the loss of money, loss of prestige and fame, and ultimately they will be reduced to a stage of no redemption.

These people are also, they fail to recognize their basic " Thamasik nature " and make no effort to change their behavior or belief system. These people have to be mentored and guided by somebody, to help them to come out of their self generated pity and self defeat tendencies.

THE SATVIKS:

The Saatvik nature people are very balanced in their emotions, and they will not overreact to any situation. They are calculated and willing to do follow the rules and conditions, to be successful. The "satvik" persons are always at peace with themselves, and they will not be agitated by the external pressures or influences.

Being Satvik means, moderation in food habits and moderation in external desires and moderation in the acquiring the materialistic things.

They are capable of recognizing their emotions and can modulate their voice and control their anger in spite of provocation. These people would prefer to spend their life without much tension and prefer peaceful living by pursuing less stressful jobs or professions.

But, we find very few people having this divine qualities of this Saatvik nature, which is very much essential for living a stress-free life and enjoy the happiness, in whatever activity, we do.

But the most important thing to observe is what is our basic or innate nature and how we are reacting to certain situations. How do we interact with people and situations. What is our mental state, whenever something is happened, beyond our expectations. How is our behavior with the society.

This type of keen observation and scrutiny will make us aware of our basic nature and we should strive to improve gradually to reach the stage of Satvik nature, if we prefer to live happily.

We have to change our behavior pattern and moderate our desires and control our negative emotions, so that we can get the control over our mind and ultimately get control on our way of thinking.

Hence, we strive to make a habit ... to be happy, whatever may be the external disturbance or situation. We have to take oath that we develop a positive attitude to look at things from a right perspective, whatever may be the provocation.

We have to strongly believe that every adverse condition or every temporary defeat will teach us some lesson which will bring us ultimate happiness in our life. We have to strongly believe that any defeat or any failure is only temporary, and it is one of the several steps to reach the final goal.

The failures are stepping stones of our success. Failure is not an opposite word for success. It is part of the process of reaching success.

If you prepare yourself for minor setbacks or initial road blocks, there is no dissatisfaction or fear of failure.

When you change your mind and prepare for initial teething trouble, you are prepared for the worse result at the same time, you are confident of winning , by continuing the efforts and overcoming the initial setbacks. When you tune your mind to be positive, nothing seems to be difficult, nothing seems to be unhappy. It is your inner software that is programming your mind and linking happiness or unhappiness to an event.

SO YOU ARE THE ARCHITECT, BUILDER OF YOUR DESTINY OR HAPPINESS.

NOT THE BLIND FAITH, NOT THE RITUALS OR POOJA, WHICH WILL CREATE YOUR DESTINY OR HAPPY STATE OF MIND.

BUT YOUR INNER PEACE AND HAPPINESS WILL ULTIMATELY DECIDE YOUR LEVEL OF COMFORT AND STATE OF HAPPINESS. IT IS ALREADY THERE. ONLY THING IS YOU ARE NOT AWARE OF IT. ONCE YOU DISCOVER IT, THERE IS NO

REASON FOR GRIEF OR MISERY.

YOU ARE ALREADY HAVING THE QUALITIES OF THE KING. BUT UNFORTUNATELY, WE FAIL TO Realize THE TRUTH.

CHAPTER SEVEN

CHOICE OR CHANCE?

Many of our troubles starts from our belief that something external, may be our birth star or position of our house, or horoscope of our spouse or birth of our children etc .. is responsible for our present position of richness or poorness, and for our success or failure.

Many of our beliefs and convictions are evolutionary in nature, and they are being nurtured and molded by our background, our education, society around us, etc.

The belief system or superstitions are injected by our parents, teachers, friends etc., who are responsible for our shaping our inner world and thought process. The society and the surrounding will add fuel to the age-old superstitions, and we will never come out those strong mental programming done by our near and dear, right from our childhood to the young age. It has firmly rooted, and we are being virtually controlled by our mental program and belief system.

A snake may be a poisonous or dangerous creature here in India, and it may be viewed as a food item in China. Presence of a cat may be sign of omen to somebody, and it may be a sign of luck to others.

A white dress is a dress code for sadness to some people, and the same may be a sign of happiness to some other people.

How you look at a thing and How you look at the world depend upon your vision or color of your glasses through which you are looking at. The same object appears differently, if you look at it through with different medium.

The object is the same, but different people view it differently, with the help of their relative reference material or medium of their vision, which is implanted or setup in the mind, at the early age.

Every person mind is conditioned and programmed by the surrounding society.

If the society believes that a house facing East brings him wealth and happiness, every person who buys that argument will try to get a house facing east only. Similarly, any superstition or belief system, creates an undeniable print on his mental fabric, and he is guided by that belief system.

For many generations, we were led to believe that we are destined to suffer, because of your sins in the earlier lives, or it is your destiny written on our head, by some unknown "GOD".

Nobody has encouraged us to change our mental attitude and nobody has told us that we are all given the same opportunities and abilities to live happily, if we could change our mindset.

We were told to adjust to our fate and accepts the misery as our misfortune.

We were snubbed or suppressed whenever we question about the blind practices and rituals.

Furthermore, we were again tutored and made to believe that whatever is happened to us, it is happened because of our fate or destiny. We are not allowed to challenge it. We are never allowed to grow beyond our present state of mind to question the authenticity of these age-old traditions.

Lack of awareness or lack of proper knowledge about our inner self is the main reason for our present unhappiness.

If at all, there is any limitation or boundary to our happiness that is imposed by us only. You alone are responsible for your present state of affairs. You are only responsible for what you are.

The Gita heralds that whatever you firmly believe about yourself. That is true. Because your inner mind, or intellect is reflecting in your thinking, words and action.

HENCE LIVE BY CHOICE NOT BY CHANCE.

TAKE THE CHANCE OF CHANGING YOUR THINKING TODAY ONLY.

Lord Krishna advised Arjuna... you are responsible for your actions. Without action you will not get any result... either it is good or bad.

CHAPTER EIGHT

AHAM BRAHMASMI(I AM THE GOD)

Every ancient scripture and Upanishads, irrespective of religion, proclaims that

AHAM BRAHAMSMI-- I AM THE GOD... YOU ARE PART AND PARCEL OF GOD.

The smallest particle of Atom is also part of the Universe.

It proclaims that there is spectacular power of God or manifestation of power of God in every living being, and it has to be tapped and awakened to realize your true potential.

Don't limit yourself that you are an ordinary immortal. You are part of this cosmos, this mighty universe and part of the great creation of God.

By nature, every human being is "chidananda Swaroopa" (every happy state) .

Happiness is the original state of human being.

That is why, when we are infants or in early childhood, we will laugh and ever cheerful, irrespective of wealth or poverty.

After certain age, we acquire all negative feelings or emotions like hatred, jealousy, possessiveness, lust etc. which will ultimately overpower of capacity to laugh and enjoy the greatness of our life. we will be programmed to believe that it is our fate to suffer. We are so mesmerized and drugged that we can not challenge the sermons and try to come out of our self-made chains.

It is not your luck or chance, but your choice of your decisions that change your destiny.

It is your own date with your abilities, your thoughts, your inner engineering that is going to show the path of happiness and eternal bliss from the jungle of self afflicted wounds of ignorance, superstitions, customs etc.

God help those help themselves. No lazy person has so far enjoyed his life. No action -no result.

So start your journey of self realization and break the chains of doubt, limits etc and explore the path of success and happiness without any doubt.

To Conclude

Happiness is inside. It is a reflection of your inner state. You are born happy.

It is your natural status to be happy. But your pursuit of happiness ends, when you realize your inner happiness and bliss.

It is your imagination of outer world and things, that creates the stress and tension.

change your outlook, change your thoughts and action to find out real happiness.

Aham Brahmsmi. I am the God. Realize your real personality and truth.

Focus on improving your inner personality and you will find the road map of happiness.

Printed by Libri Plureos GmbH in Hamburg,
Germany